The Other Tree

The Other Tree
Copyright © 2025 ALISON LUBAR

For permissions and information on ordering books, contact operations@smallharborpublishing.com.

Cover design: Diana Baltag
Back cover author photo: Jay Shifman
Interior design: Claire Eder
Editor: Beth Bolton
Publisher: Allison Blevins
Press Director: Kristiane Weeks-Rogers
Managing Editor: Bianca Dagostino

THE OTHER TREE
ALISON LUBAR
ISBN 978-1-957248-55-4
Harbor Editions,
an imprint of Small Harbor Publishing

The Other Tree

Poems from Pre-Internment, Onward

Alison Lubar

Harbor Editions
Small Harbor Publishing

For us

Contents

Foreword by Maya Williams

Alison Lubar's *THE OTHER TREE: Poems from Pre-Internment, Onward* is a remarkable read of specified and vaguely specified ekphrasis of nonlinear time (including the future) that connects feminine Japanese lineage, strawberries, navigating poverty and racism, hidden and visible bruises, good rice and bad rice, and surviving as untamed Japanese femmes and women.

A "self-swaddle" filled with triptych, sonnet, haibun, contrapuntal, prose poem, brackets/parenthetical, and more, *THE OTHER TREE* is simultaneous time travel and witness of variety of the now.

As a Black multiracial poet, I understand how exhausting it may be to read narratives of light-skinned multiracial writers. However, through Lubar's contextualization of generational multiracial identity and their whole family's confrontation with Japanese internment camps, this collection is anything but exhausting.

Where it's easy to be the black sheep in settings that reject the speaker, they are a wolf. A wolf tabulating the people to righteously hate that harms them and their family. A wolf that craves to bite their heads off with every disposal of great food and every racist joke or impersonation. Reclaiming the animal inside because "local wildlife doesn't discriminate."

The wildlife includes the plants with thorns, strawberries, raspberries, and lemons as images throughout. A baptism of lemons at where you call home is better than a baptism of a prison under the euphemism of "relocation."

THE OTHER TREE showcases that home is not just in a place or in people, home is what remains after we're gone. "Trans-generational grief engenders both/tenderness and bitterness." Grief also teaches us how to build and hold space for ongoing roots, as seen in the collection's title poem about the tree outside the speaker's aunt's home:

Beneath this other family tree, I re-enter the narrative. Entwine these words
like nascent roots, thread through backyard dirt and last year's leaves. Even if

she sells this house to a predatory tenant, even if this is the last time I share
the air with her and this, I will always trace myself back here.

I'm grateful to have selected Alison Lubar's poetry collection for Harbor Editions' Laureate Prize. I hope you all enjoy what their poems have in store for you.

—*Maya Williams, 1/5/25*

The Other Tree

*"Life is not what you alone make it.
Life is the input of everyone who
touched your life and every experience
that entered it. We are all part of one another."*

*"Not everything is taught to us
in school. It's up to us to find out."*

"transform yourself first"

—Yuri Kochiyama

(Re)Generation Triptych (1940-2019)

I. Auntie, Picking Strawberries in May (1940)

While they were picking strawberries,
I was listening for screams.

Every fifteen minutes,
as often as I would try to wait to run
to the bathroom to wash the sticky witness
of poverty from my hands,
the manual labor of a ten-year-old,
   I would listen for the screams
of women in the field
who came across
a garter snake.
   Helpless, the snake,
and helpless, the women,
and helpless, us who waited
   for a December
   to change our lives—

but for now, I pinch the strong,
thin stem and place
each freckled reminder of my life
in a basket.
   I save the good ones for the top,
   and the bruised sweat underneath,
   blemished by no fault of their own.

I am not unhappy. I wait for the screams,
better at picking snakes than strawberries.

II. Smile Like You Mean It (2018)

The divorces my grandmothers never got
materialize thirty-three years later in the same
place they suffered the most (but isn't every
suburbanite in that state?).
                                        Each stayed
and never smiled: whole photo albums
of frowns, taught lips over hidden teeth,
early lines from not laughing are all
ash now, or interred in concrete. I mirror
them in dimpled chin, slope of nose,
freckled cheekbones catching sadness.

But the great-aunt who never married
      grew crows' feet by thirty
from gleeful freedom: eternally
      bachelorette and feral.

I visit her mid-separation
and wonder if her nonagenarian
      wisdom will give me her selective hearing, or pity.

Who am I without this wound?

Auntie replies, "You are Samurai,"
and that is enough of a vote, affirmation
to veto my own diffidence as the half-blind
      calico licks melted ice cream from a ramekin,
behind the cardboard partition erected
      around the only extra placemat, and matches
Auntie's wrinkled cheshire grin.

III. It Will Be a Garden Again (2019)

Last year's tomato vines' hollow bones snap,
a satisfactory breaking. Cannibalized for compost,
they barely shatter: each shaft bereft of marrow,

hollow—the garden's heart is a cavern,
dried vines splinter like brittle ventricles.
This is how I winnow you from memory:

our roots easily relinquish dirt—
no fine fibers of life left to cling
to this body of Earth we built.

Ungrounded, unburied, it scatters
all of *us*, in a new season's wind,
warm enough for garter snakes,
the neighbor's tabby—every wanderer
finding temporary respite, with permanent
room for   just me   and the bees.

I leave the untidy strawberries,
wayward   tendrils   spilling   out
of chicken wire onto pebbled path—
you wanted to uproot them (*too wild*),
split vines like ancestral veins. I let them
grow to the lawn   and   over the walkway—

I am both immersed conservator and distant witness,
lucky that something untamed   and   sweet   survives.

Elementary Lesson

Tule Lake Relocation Center, 1943

Everything is a test. The teachers
patrol the aisles of makeshift desks. No
Catholic-school ruler or pointer to snap
at a left-hand, just listening for us
to denounce the US. Any infidelity
is treason. Do not even draw the sun.
Any of us could be spies—even us,
fifth graders. Cursive tendrils leave
chalky ghost-dust after each lesson.
With one swipe, the day is erased. It takes
just one puff of air from ruddy ballooned cheeks
for a name to disappear.

Superior(ity) Complex(ion)
Oakland CA, 2009

Auntie says, "Jack was handsome
to European girls, but among us,
he was a dime a dozen." He shrinks
each year. Turns to prune. Refuses
to return my mother's letters. Then
loses each of us as a spring branch
snipped before its buds unfurl. Like
so many losses of names overseas.
Whole cities. At least two. And here,
three years of camps. When Auntie
says, "I'm glad they lost the war,"
she means that no one wins when
families disintegrate into poverty, or
into mere atoms. Auntie says, "The good
die young. That's why I've made it
to my eighties."

Auntie, Cross-Country

U.S. Highway 66, 1961

Pocketbooks full
of scribbled digits
on bar napkins, we flee
each dive with a wink
and a wave (we'll never
give *them* a call). Our green
Beetle revs and peels—
we *told them* it had wings!

I roll down one glass eye
while Leona coaxes flight—
we merge and she takes it up
twenty more as the gasoline trail
of station wagons & eighteen-
wheelers sweeten the air.

"Eat our dust!"
we whip past a last
pickup-truck—
in the rearview it
shrinks to a blip
on Route 66.

Tonight, there are three
new notes, turned to
a flurry of twenty-ish—
the age we seem (joy
ingests crows' feet
like a delicacy).

We dance everywhere we go:
freedom's foliage
is a flutter
of numbers.

Pancakes with Ojisan
Somewhere Pennsylvania, 1993

I slide down the tiny blue-plastic desk chair
and risk the static, shrinking into my seat
as Mrs. Wilson announces
        "Pancake breakfast with grandparents!"
And I think first,
        No one looks like Oji.
And I think second,
        I only have one person to bring.
And that day, I do.

My blue-eyed, curly-haired
Bonnema [her ashes interred
under Belgian sky, in sun-warmed
concrete, topping a hill of wild perennials]
would have joined willingly,
in raspberry velour jogging suit
and mink coat. And I'm here
[with her worse half] wishing
Oji whiter.

I knew that as soon as they discovered
I have no *grandpa, pop-pop,* or *poppy,*
the ["classroom flirt"] boys draw up
the corners of their eyes
with middle fingers: I am
no longer mere brunette,
summer-darkened, but
reborn as "other."

I could blend in until now. [This family betrayal
is not the first.] I use my index finger and thumb
to widen my eyes, top to bottom, and stick my tongue out
at the same boys, and almost receive a principal's office referral.

[Six months later, no one eats Mom's yakitori
at the classroom cultural celebration, either.]

Only twenty years after do I think of how
Oji must have felt a familiar othering, a routine

gauntlet of gazes. The other kids' third-grade
*Grand*parents probably would have made
the same, stupid face, and would have also
not gotten in any trouble.

That day, we sat in silence, mutilating
pancakes with white-plastic fork sides
[since knives are dangerous]. Each syrupy bite,
drenched in a maple imposter, reminds me
that nothing is ever [special and] different
in a good way.

The King of Horses
Edison NJ, 2013

Horse bites never bruise. Your index and middle finger
curl to fangs, knuckles turn into the mandible of the beast
little girls never think their ponies will grow up to be—
or Black Beauty, who lost use of a limb and then his life,
useless because there's no majesty in standing with a crutch.

The horse bites from Ojisan were nothing
compared to what other little girls might have suffered
from a long line of lost pride and a grasping for power.

I never saw you in hospice, at the veteran's hospital,
in a British suit and beret, cigar, and nothing to note
you're Japanese except your eyes and skin and nails;
nothing to belie the ancestral line of samurai. I can't
imagine you any smaller, as you must have been
eighteen years ago, when I was ten—the last time
I saw you. You filled out the plastic lawn chair,
yellow plaid woven seat and back around
the hollow aluminum frame.

You'd sit in my parents' driveway, like a king,
afraid of owning anything yourself. The apartment
you shared with Bonnema temporary enough to let you
think of leaving, but you went from nothing special
among girls to the exotic and dark, handsome and dashing,
"The Oriental Fred Astaire" they called you.
And I'm still exotic, too, and so lucky, too, to seem
so foreign and dangerous and willing to bite.

MoonShine

Tacoma WA, 1930

Jack's face shimmers

                               veil of cold sweat over

the vat of moonshine,

nose scrunched   like the noble folktale rabbit.

He puffs up, ruffles

                          small muscles in a white

undershirt to stand in front

of his mother, little sister, little

brother. He is thrown across the room

         again.   The rabbit throws himself

                                   into the fire.

He decides to become a bear.   The rabbit becomes the moon.

It's called a shiner, a black eye.   Every night,

the same pageant. Every night,   the rabbit appears

                              less and less.

Art Imitates Life
Antwerp & Edison, 1932-1992

Here's the difference—the opalescent bowl
lives at the country house, atop a smaller mantle
than the main Antwerp address. Her husband would
spend a childhood picking strawberries instead of
painting them. Sweat shimmering on an upper lip,
sunburned cheeks just as red.

The towels in my grandparents' bathroom
were the same color as the tile, walls, tub:
pink and acidic. Phosphorescent frosted glass lamps
and my grandfather's dark back awaiting a boar-bristle brushing.
In the cluttered back room, two twins made an uncomfortable king.
Visiting, at six, with my mother, I'd roll to the middle rift to get closer
after I'd struggle through Dr. Seuss. Now, I imagine my own
mother at seven, rolling into the soft, white arms of her own.
In the morning, learning to paint freckles on fruit, smoothing over
all blemishes—all the brown, rotting bruises.

Derivative Curriculum
Public School PA 2001

"Of course we teach essential texts" he lies
to my mother and father on back-to-school night.
Because the curriculum is easy and scripted already
and not much has happened since. At least
many of us fail to make a change in economy,
liberty. Who has those taken away?
My calculus teacher pulls back
the corners of his eyes to tell a joke,
to reel us in. I feign ineptitude, fail tests.
The principal swears this couldn't have happened
because everybody loves him. In first grade I make a list
of people I hate and my teacher calls my parents. I try to be
unlikeable. I come home to declare, "I am not
a sheep," to be the one to separate myself,
claim "the other." All the while, the shame
sticks in my throat like a salmon swimming
upstream, before it's clubbed out of the water. We
never read *Farewell to Manzanar*, I still can't measure
limits at infinity, and I continue to add their names.

They called my mother
Edison NJ, 1961

"chink" the first time when she was ten. It was
before there was anyone mixed like her
almost anywhere. She would dye
everything in groovy swirls using
the turkey pan. It made no sense,
this insult. "I'm not even Chinese,"
she explains, fifty-four years later.
Community is being anti-war
at the end of high school. "There was
one Chinese boy who was a freshman,
and I told the other kids to scram." No one
would ignore her then, willowy and long,
oil slick-dark hair, perfect long pink ovals
of nails, like translucent bivalves. Sex appeal
is a weapon she taught me to wield
by fifteen. No one has called me that, yet,
to my face.

Self Portrait in a Type of Mirror
Suburban PA, 1990

We sketch each other, sit knee-to-knee.
I am six. My mother is still postpartum,

another loss. I am once again an only
child. I know faces are circles. A neck

is a rectangle. Use the side of the pencil
for thick hair. The point makes tiny wisps.

Leave a white oval in the pupil—to imitate
cartoons. Everything looks better in my head.

On paper, she smiles, close-lipped, a little
fallen comma at each corner. No wrinkles

because I love her today. I know it's bad.
I know she'll say it's great. She uses

charcoal. I never realized she gave me
eyelashes, too. Now, they're here forever.

I am always this small and pretty, to her. All
in black and white. Everything greyscale.

Eyes are already rounded like teardrops.
Her basement art room is chilly for Spring,

and I can bear only ten minutes until I have
to crawl into her lap. I am too young to know

the heart has no easy shape.

"You can't say 'Oriental'"
Suburban Pennsylvania, 1994

because it's offensive." My blue-eyed friend
sneers, smiles at superiority in knowledge,
fairness, and freckles. My mother says
her hair is mousy.

My mother is not a rug. She has used
this word for forty years, feels its reclaimed
East-Asian kinship. This word is hers; it is
mine. She taught me to

I. *"find / establish / feel one's bearings / location / way, get the lie of the land"*
as other, as not-them—unbelonging
at the lunchbox cracked open.
Fourth grade culture day potluck
leaves yakitori untouched. I throw
it out of blue tupperware into the bushes—
local wildlife doesn't discriminate, and relay
its evaporation with delight: "they loved it."

II. *"adapt, accommodate, acclimatize, attune"*
I learn to accommodate questions until
I'm thirty. I acclimatize to exotic. Attune
to scrutiny. I do mind you asking; I do
not exist to satiate curiosity. This unease
others you; I sniff it in like sweet gasoline.
I will respond with fire. Like her, I am crowned
with midnight river hair so long, it tucks into our jeans.
We belong everywhere.

III. *"aim, steer, design, intend"*
toward mysterious as a hand I hold
to chest. Or a ship adrift, I outmaneuver
and drop into the conversation my Auntie,
the camps, Godzilla—what's *of my people.*
Use chopsticks for popcorn, cheese crackers,
anything oily. Scoff at weight control advice:
"they'll help you eat slower!" unless you've
always used them. She still keeps
my pink plastic baby ones with birds,

19

little finger loops for a toddler.

IV. *"align, place, position, set"*
My mother as direction, I fix my sight
where the sun rises: eastward. She
warms me face first.

Only Bonnema
Edison NJ, 1996

is missing
        in this apartment. Ancient make-
                up spread across the low bureau
        for a makeshift vanity. I only use
cakey blue and stodgy red. (Once,
        I filled in a whole coloring book
                with just spring-sky eyelids and
        macintosh apple pouts.) I accompany
my mom to the Asian market with a full
        face of paint. Today, she doesn't wipe it off.
                I get a whole tub of lychee jellies. I ask for
        a new tea set. (I test my mother's grief.)
It comes in a painted cardboard box
        with fuchsia polyester lining. I never
                use it, and the jellies sit on top of the fridge
        three years past expiration. Soon there is
nothing left in the freezer that's hers, either.
        (No summer tomato soup, no blueberry pie,
                no rainy-day brioche dough.) Jack will not
        go hungry because he's still handsome
enough. Strangers see a sweet widower.
        A parade of old-world girlfriends feed
                his ego, too. (They don't know to take him
        to the Asian market.) My mother and I
        sort sweater sets and home-sewn
wiggle dresses. (They still sit in my parents' basement closet.)
        I take the makeup. (I never
        use it again.) We miss her
        arms the most.

Jack as Botanical Triptych
Edison NJ, 1970

One
As a cerulean impressionist iris, from another
neglected schizophrenic who paints in waves
like Hokusai. Another influenced by the East
(my mother would say "Orientals"). Draped silk
spans shoulder to shoulder, a mantle of grief. Just
a turning of head would fold the hollow stems
irreparably. Does it still smell like cigars? Of dark
aviators and bleached undershirts as you sit
in my parents' driveway like it's your own?
You didn't need to risk a mortgage. It's easier
to flee month to month. Uproot. We perennials
always find a way to still bloom.

Two
There must have been some trust
in staying. Raspberry bushes along
the apartment complex fence. Of course
you'd want a fruit with thorns. Though
you refused the kitchen otherwise,
you'd concoct ice cream with raspberry
syrup. It freezes with shards—even dessert
is sharp, but still delicious.

Three
Once, you were so cruel, my mother stabbed you with a salad fork.
Its prongs stuck in hard belly fat, its handle bounced like a cartoon
diving board, or popsicle stick garden-row markers in March wind.
I don't know what happened next, except, at that moment you knew
that one day you, too, would return to earth, interred.

Love can look like
Bethlehem PA, 1995

printed irises
on a silk scarf
from the museum
giftshop, Irish wool
berets, three cards
on my birthday, the other two
from the grandmothers
when they couldn't write anymore.
Sitting in the front seat. Offering me
the cheek and eyeball of ginger-steamed fish.
My mother taking you out of our lives,
like a fish hook in a gaping, slippery mouth.

To another girl, called "other":
South Jersey, Public School, 2018

they can't figure out
how to make fun of you,
so they fall in love. You

are a scatterplot—no primary
color, no neat column of statistics;
this combination leaves you

alien and otherworldly like
the gods, face of all humanity
because they all see themselves
reflected in you, but not enough

to feel like you're one of them.

It's not a haunting, but a reign
Suburban PA, 2018

Shizuko floats from the bedroom
bookcase shelf with its pantheon

of silver frames. This is no
formal altar. Her kimono wet-

bottomed from ethyl alcohol
bathtub rice wine dabbles a path

that evaporates, leaving more
in the air than on the yellow carpet

of my childhood bedroom. "Let me
tell you how we were also descended

from a Korean princess." This was
only a deathbed confession, before.

"Mr. Martin let me clean his house
after the camps. He said, *Your people*

lost the war. What do you have
to live for, here?" We have something

to live for everywhere. She wafts
back up, a boozy trail. "They all still

crossed the street for years. Pity is
always part of fear."

YellowThroat
Tule Lake, 1944

This discarded fence post piece will become
a bird. Out of all of Audubon's dog-eared pages
she chooses the common yellowthroat,
wonders at a golden voice, a warbler.
Black stripe across the eyes
for its nickname of the yellow bandit.
            She remembers a Shakespearean
            mother as a wren. She remembers, too,
            the son before his throat is cut. Before this,
            he promises to survive. The mother asks,
      "And what will you do now? How will you live?"
And he says, "As birds do, mother."
"What, with worms and flies?"
"With what I get, I mean; and so do they."
            The mother leaves this scene
            screaming. In the next one,
            she's already dead.
        Both mothers wonder
     what lives they held before they gave
     life to everything after. Does this statuette
remember being a fence? Does the bird
remember the egg? The first lesson that safety, too,
is fragile? Why yellow and not gold?
            Sunset bandit. Buttercup thief.
     Now the yellowthroat remembers
     being a tree. She remembers freedom
     the same way. Michelangelo is said to have
     seen angels in marble.
            His work was merely
            to set them free. In eighty years, her grand-
            daughter will retire and watch these
            from her sunny backyard deck, will have
            a husband to install a heated birdbath
            for the winter, to keep the birds coming—
to continue the show, unseasonably.
     For now, she uses a pocket knife
            to take long curls, and saves them
                 for fire starting; creates tinder, too,
                   just in case, to burn all

she cannot scream.

Generational Demons as Indigestion
Suburban NJ, 2022

"The rice was bad"
is a euphemism—
she has no bitterness.

Two glasses of prosecco
in a row turns to pins jumbling
in a tarnished peppermint tin.

I'll do anything not to throw up.
Bad stomachs are hereditary.
Auntie outlived the cancer. I get

little patches of scales. I am too nervous
to heal. There, they poisoned the rice. Here,
they don't need to bother. Any grandmother knows

flat ginger ale will neutralize norovirus. Saltine crackers
are the holy body that keeps intestinal peace. Really,
I don't feel that bad.

It skips a generation
Suburban Pennsylvania, 2015

I'm home for a funeral and sift through photographs.
The plastic tub with the warning that people could
suffocate if you seal them in with the lid, filled
with images of my mother as a child, and her mother,

and Jack. I still want to call him Oji but showing
that I know he's in me and in my own cruelty
is a cruelty I can't show to my mother, who
suffered the most under him.

I hear tales of his handsomeness from his sister,
from his girlfriend (though we never call her that),
and he seems so harmless in the pictures from the beach.

Handsome is never harmless. My mother, a toddler,
maybe older, holding a plastic shovel. Everything is grey,
but I imagine the red swimsuit and blue-green sea. I flip through.
Striped swimsuits and smiling. He couldn't have been that mean.

And then I see, second to last, my mother's four-year-old face
frozen in terror in her backward glance at Jack. I shouldn't want
anyone to look at me like that. But I know I inherit it all.

Inedible

Suburban PA, 1991

When Ojisan horse bites, turns his knuckles to teeth,
to catch my soft, pre-teen upper thigh, Bonnema wields

a snappy plastic-bottomed slipper as aegis. We all have
matching white bunny ones: her, my mother, and me.

Polyester wooly faces with a little pink triangle nose.
Barely space for toes. Mine are so brown next to them.

My mother warns, *Don't get too dark!* like I don't belong
this bronzed. *Phenotype is fate*—damn genetic destiny.

The world won't ever really change, so best to water
it down; best to dilute even if all that's left is mud.

Runoff from rinsing acrylic brushes. My mother buys me
a stone bracelet to ground, protect. The chakras are really

plastic-coated glass beads. They flake a rainbow, leave
milky translucence, lack any magic. But tiger's eye is real.

Brown, warm, striated, golden stone. I'd still prefer that
to the expected edibles: chocolate, rum, caramel, cinnamon.

Describing any part of a person that way implies that everything,
everyone melanated is consumable. The world is full of cannibals.

My mother and mother's mother would blanche me, keep
the almond eyes set in a marble face, unloved by sun. But Oji

instead let me darken—like him. Even each pinch was a wish, to turn
softness to steel, something bitter and sharp and always ready to bite,

or at least break your teeth.

Trompe L'oeil, le Cœur
Bethlehem PA, 1993

I always think the rice is ice cream,
double take at the perfect scoops
in a silver bowl. It might be a vase.
I am not completely disappointed.
When I'm warned I might not like some-
thing I trick myself to trick them. Yes, jelly-
fish is a noodle from the sea. Broccoli is
my favorite part of this. I learn to be
unexpected. I let Oji
drop the fish cheek
on my plate but let a squirm
escape at the sight of the next
delicacy: the eyeball. He teases
but not to be cruel
this time. Love is
saving the best
parts for someone
else. Even when
it looks like some-
thing else.

Sukiyaki [before migration]
Oakland CA, 1961

I.

Granny slices into creminis, eight-pointed stars, cuts carrot coins into buttercups, each enoki thread tangles with watercress. We cut the bitterness with rich dashi and marbled beef. Her nails, like tiny bivalves, flutter atop the butcher block, snipping napa cabbage into fine strips, tender inner leaves shredded to a nest.

II.

I, her round-eyed granddaughter, have her feathery hair at my temples—downy wisps of brown mimic her grey.

III.

This is the first time she lets me help. I peel each oyster mushroom from its cluster, fan them on my own cutting board, gills down, like she always does. She nods and hands me a yellow paring knife, zipping the air down with a thumb to show me how to cut—right down the middle. Surgical precision. With a flick of her wrist, the ingredients dance into the pot.

IV.

I mimic the same, mirror her music, watch my handiwork half-slip into the gas burner. Granny's hands come underneath mine, and we shoo the rest into the bubbling, become one four-winged bird, fluttering through on the fragrant steam.

[Quapa] Imposter Syndrome
Cherry Hill NJ, 2014

When they [only]
       bring me
a fork at Ichiban,
       I feel home
leaving my body.

The Body of Grief as Rice and Butter

A body, from a body, from a body, from a body. Trans-generational grief engenders both tenderness and bitterness. Since their incarceration during the Japanese Internment, my grandfather, his sister, and their mother have processed this trauma in ways that have affected my mother and me. Each of us have broken some cycle; all of these broken rings still rattle around somewhere. Is each more like a link on a necklace or chainmail? And just because there's an opening doesn't mean that it's ever lost.

I have Auntie's badge from the camps. Its brittle plastic coating holds a yellowed photo of her at thirteen. We were both chubby in the same ways. Now, she has begun to fold into herself, eighty-four years later. She is the last one left, and has lived the longest. Everyone else was eaten from the inside—stomach cancer from the asbestos rice, or stroke from refusing to eat anything without butter.

The butter is not to blame. Neither is the rice. I eat them together, mixed in my little red rice maker from Target. It was less than twenty bucks. Its nonstick coating scratched from white roommates using tablespoons to scrape generic long grain onto their plates. You have to use something wooden, at least, to part the starchy bottom from the pot. Left overnight, a translucent veil covers the sides. That means I didn't rinse it enough. If it was still laced with talc to prevent sticking, this would kill me in twenty more years. And nonstick coating is a rumored carcinogen—there are many ways of slow implosion.

How do I keep all these little parts inside? What remains? Scent is the strongest sense tied to memory, but forsaking Proust's madeleines, I conjure apricot cookies, matcha mochi, even potato chips, which go best with prosecco. I eat my way back to love and through loss. I imagine everyone I've lost not as grey dust, but something metaphysical that sticks somewhere. And sometimes begins to grow. If you are what you eat, I am all memory.

My mother is sad today, so
A Delaware Beach, 2021

I collect shells for her, these shore-
       line shards with sea-smoothed
wounds for string, a tinkling mobile
       of soprano trill to recall also baritone
shushing of waves, like a heartbeat
       in utero. Each hole shows the way
a soft bivalve succumbs to seagull,
       shows every treasure carries a history
of loss. I wrap us in this iridescence,
       pearly and palm-shaped, hidden in flinty
grey. I collect twelve to bead on turquoise string.
       I promise I'll make something beautiful
out of something discarded,
       this time, for her.

Catch and Release
Suburban PA, 1992

On Mother's Day, dad takes Oji fishing
to leave us three at home. You can tell the Flemish
by our chins, strong jaw, and a little bump
like a nub of brioche. In the photo from this day,
we all half-smile, my sharp-cut preschool bangs.
I'm grateful I was spared the bowl cut. What else
is there to do but create? We roll out the pale,
chilled dough, the edges flare in small crags.
They let me use the little zig-zag wheel to cut
diamonds. I know this is kind and patient
and my precision is the best I can do. It feels a shame
to discard the edges so they let me shape them
into little cat faces. One dollop of apricot jam,
fold the edges to hug it in. As we wait for the click
of the oven to preheat the garage door rumbles.
A whole styrofoam cooler of perch tumbles
into the sink, ice slides over green bodies. It doesn't smell like death
yet. Pond-bottom overbears the sweetness of twenty minutes ago.
We three wait in the dining room for them to finish. How can I choose
whose lap I climb into? My mother defers to hers. We are all still dusted
in flour, passive and Rubenesque, waiting for the kitchen
violence to cease, the blunt-edge scrape against scales
to stop, for the reward of something sweet and free.

Just Desserts

Tennessee, 1970

In the Smoky Mountains, I am sober.
The skid stops, tires grind on gravel,

the path whorled and looped like
a fingerprint. I almost go over. The edge

is right there. Climb to the empty passenger's side
and slide down. A little black sedan pulls over,
someone in billowing paisley opens the door.

I spill like a tipped laundry basket, a pile of denim
and silk. I pull the red bandana over my eyes—

it matches the VW Bug, matches what might have filled
the inside if we went over. I can see how my car
and I could just splat. "There must be a reason,"

my impromptu EMT trills. "I'm going
to eat dessert for breakfast every day
from now on." We laugh and survey

the external damage—none to see,
and inside of me there's a seed

of possibility now, that I will replant
in everyone I meet.

Autie, Refusing Baptism

Tule Lake Relocation Center, 1944

"The straight and narrow
was no life for me.

Not wanting to disappoint
my mother, but only the pastor,
I refused baptism.

      How could I live
the straight and narrow
      when I preferred
the wide and winding?

The path trampled and fed
with tributaries and branching
off to another place.

I didn't want a road, or even a map.
And besides, we couldn't even leave
the camp."

Writing the Wrongs
Tacoma WA, 1941

Every Monday before the camps,
Jack pawns the typewriter. This cash
is for rice, greens, any fatty meat
to flavor it all. Enough for two little
siblings, a mother. Father gone
to somewhere else for work,
a relief. No use in making
moonshine now. In the mornings,
he delivers newspapers. Greyscale
propaganda—hate is a binary. Fear
turns black then ash in the stove.
Then logging. Jack would like to
write, not cut. Make the words,
not dole them out, or demolish
the towering hemlocks that may turn
to pages one day. I imagine that
the Saturday buy-back gives him
enough time to pull those stories
from the ether, or whatever hovers
over him before he is a prisoner
of an additional, different type.

Before Any Binary
Suburban PA, 1989

I know no difference between me
and the other preschool kids except

that I was taught to color in the lines.
Lips are always red, eyelids like sky.

I fill whole books with these two shades.
I use both hands to pour from a pitcher,

and know which wooden blocks support
the highest towers. I sit mostly still,

and swing my legs under the table.
Simon Says is easy. Listening is a first
access to power and safety. The best

fruit snack is the blue T-Rex. Yellow
pterodactyls taste nothing like lemons.
Nothing compares to Bonnema's blueberry pie.

She places it on the lowest shelf of the fridge
so I can sample the middle before dinner.

The lattice crust holds so much love.
Each purple pinch of honeyed middle

stains my index and thumb. No one
tells me not to. I am the guiltless culprit,

with three and a half sets of arms to run to.
Even Oji is still sweet, for at least another year.

One More and You're Out

Oakland CA, 2014

Two strikes are good for a pitcher and bad for a dog—
the orange warning in the bay window watches
the sheepdog-nemesis pass at six every day.

The inside sill is shredded with the desperate scratches
of Pepper, rescued Aussie mix and resident antagonist.
Auntie sews canvas blackout panels with lemons and eagles,
signs of growth and skyward escape, to shield Pepper
from this daily agitation and certain war.

Irises sprout from the bench in front, next to
the perennial rosemary we never pick—the sheepdog
marks it for his own. Pepper reclaims it—a land war.

One day, Auntie is early and the sheepdog is late—
with a primal lunge, Pepper breaks the leash, a wrist, the skin
of the enemy—and that's how strike two happened. (The first
was a shih tzu, whose response to treatment and insistence
on living spared Pepper, too.) The rescue dog and the old maid.
When no one else can bear to live with you, two negatives
cancel each other in perfect math. Pepper's last strike
was merely age. Auntie waits for her turn at bat.

An Ode on the E
Oakland CA, 2025

Auntie E keeps
the melody of the latter
letter. Aunt like on't, like
upon, not the picnic pest,
kitchen interloper, mistaken
for pepper in a dirty soup.
I would eat it anyway,
Auntie says, or shrugs and fishes
the drowning insect out,
administers microscopic
CPR. The E lives with infamy,
ineffable, eccentric. To be E,
Most of my enemies and friends
are gone, so I guess I've made
peace with the world. The most
common vowel, impossible to escape.
She persists in euphemism, *The rice*
was bad. She has no bitterness
and still takes a slice of apple galette
for breakfast. I will give her a pre-
moniker, knighted title of "Ancient"
for her second hundred years.

Après-Camp, or, Retail Therapy
San Francisco CA, 1948

New socks with yellow thread loop scalloped edges,
a spiral-bound notebook with hard cardboard cover,
then later a pack of marbled composition ones [their spots
like an aerial view of a crowded ranch and its jersey cows,
or somewhere dense, cramped and caged], a poetry collection
or any number of paperback editions small enough to stow
in a pocketbook. Seed-beaded barrettes and a [black silk]
camisole. My mother [one day, Granny] sorts through
and chooses the nicest to ship back to Japan. "They have
nothing there." I start to only buy gifts [for myself] too big
to ship. Fishermen's cabled sweaters, thick ecru knots like ships
[or gallows], encyclopedia volumes from the thrift store [I promise
myself to memorize J through K], combat boots [I choose
blue laces]. When she is gone, I revert to miniature, assemble
a dollhouse. Thimble trashcans. Bottlecap pie tins. Cork vanity
stool, complete with cotton ball tufted seat. A quilting square
for a flat sheet. I even wire its lights to flash, with a switch
[for signals]. Off, [on. Here,] gone.

The Real Prize Is to Know

Officer Candidate School, 1950

I will not be
the sacrifice
they ask. To jump
on the grenade, to
turn inside out,
back popped open
like a Christmas
cracker. My spine
as prize, vertebrae
confetti. Once, one
pushes me atop
to save himself
in this practice run,
the fake grenade
an unripened pear.
This will bruise
my lowest ribs. It's not
even a punch. This fight
is not mine to have.
And besides,
we don't celebrate
holidays anymore.

Before I know better,
Antwerp, 1995

I try. No one can stand Jack, but I still
call him Ojisan. He is charged with my care
while the other adults go to a real dinner.

We go to the hotel piano bar, Oji in wool suit,
beret, cigar. I am in dusty sandals and muted
pastel dress, bounce my bare heels on the edge

of the navy leather lounge chair. [I will not
be like the others. I will tolerate bitter quips
and widemouth frowns.] I play dumb and quiet

and let him fill the air with grief. The maraschino
of my Shirley Temple [oh to have ringlets!]
bobs between chipped ice. [I'd like to

drink a bottle of grenadine.] I know no
moderation. I am too young [Who wouldn't
let a bathtub overflow with rosy bubbles?]

to know not to pick all of the cashews
from the silver bowl. [I leave the peanuts.]
This effusive enthusiasm is how I learned

to love [and later fake it]. Unmitigated optimism.
I am [chubby to him, but] still cute [with baby-
fat]. It is three days since Bonnema was interred.

[She died next to him.] No horse bites tonight. [I still
put my small, tanned hand on his, of the same tone.]

Solidarity
Hakone, 2009

I had had enough herding
of Auntie through Tokyo
subway. We finally arrive
at the spa after a Pirate
Cruise. We order consommé
and something suspended
in aspic. Everything hovers
here: steam, gnats, sex-
lessness. I lock eyes with
someone with their own
older someone. We shrug
and spend the night taking
trips to the 7-Eleven down the hill
for onigiri and sake in little
egg cups. We conjure Easter,
camaraderie, rebirth, and flirt.
The sun rises right on time—
he leans in and I am all
rabbit panic. Say my good-
bye and in our room, Auntie
is still up. "Now I know how
your father felt when you
were a teenager." I shower,
we never get to the spa, and
spend the whole bus ride
to Kyoto shrouded in a mix
of regret and affirmation. Some
things never change. I resume
my place to safeguard Auntie
as we usher from shrine to
shrine, avoid all indulgences
except for food. The rice is
the best here.

Nothing Skips a Generation
California Temporal-Diptych

I. 1945
When the war was over,
[on paper] it wasn't over.
There, we [became dust.
Here, we] returned to dust—
America was [a home
that held no home]
left. Even the door-
[jamb was stripped. Doors]
closed, never [to open]
for work, for us. Open
[a tin, salmon in] a can.
No [one ever can]
come back.

II. 2015
Back in the cradle of sunshine,
this state my mother and I return to, as if
it was a type of womb. [I am too much
East Coast to be patient at the grocery
when someone lingers too long
at the wall of salad mixes.] This still
isn't the place for me. [Neither is the town
where I went to school.] When I say,
"I'm going home," I mean to a person.
We return to Auntie's with little tins
of tapas, a pain d'épi from Acme,
and oranges from our neighborhood
walk. [Everyone's backyard blossoms
in citrus. They put surplus in cardboard
boxes, on the front steps, to share.] Dinner
is all snacks, all picking. Auntie lets me use
the good Belgian crystal glasses, since now
I have another college degree. [I am still not
working on a PhD, like Ishiro.] But,
when Auntie says, "You look like Jack,"
I don't take it as an insult. I respond
[with the Scottish play], "What's done
cannot be undone."

"Very cruel race,"
Oakland CA, 2001

declares an early 2000s romcom.
The bumbling starlet listens
to her dashing crush, twirls
sun-colored hair. All her cuticles are chewed.
West Coast twilight turns the two walls of windows
deep-ocean dark. Three generations of us sit
underneath the newly installed flatscreen. My mother
brings the DVD in her luggage, to give to Auntie afterwards.
Very cruel race registers
like an underwater sonic boom. I laugh
on reflex. All of us nod, and understand.
Once, Auntie beat another schoolkid
with a yellow umbrella to prevent further bullying. Cruelty
is preventative, and it's better to let people know
where they stand. No furtive poisoning of rice,
no euphemistic relocation. This is before
I come out. This self-hate, internalized,
eats away like the stomach cancer Granny
and her estranged husband died from. A coyote
that chews off a leg to escape isn't cruel. The captive
mouse that eats her pups. Fishing with a baseball bat.
Ending a marriage over the phone line of the rehab center.
At the end, the fair heroine gets her guy. Happily ever ever.

Parable of the Tiger

Suburban PA, 1998

Jack forgot my mother was born
in the year of the tiger. When she writes
that he can't see me anymore, that horse
bites hurt, that words can be even worse,
he cuts us off forever.

[No phone calls, even
from the veteran's hospital twenty years later.
She will still take his own ashes overseas,
so he can rest with Bonnema, and instead
turn his rage to her in the afterlife.]

The lined paper might as well
be marked with stripes. In long,
thin letters, cursive loops, she still
signs it with retractable claws:
"love,"

Something (Hidden and) Blue (Abides)
New Jersey, 2015

Mining my underwear drawer for forgotten costume jewelry
the grey velvet clamshell of a box,
no bigger than a child's palm emerges
as I brush away the thongs I never wear.

Unopened since it served as something blue,
Bonnema's aquamarine rests in darkness.

The hinge cracks,
the creak of 50 years in the jewelry business
and the inside still smells like her
white and coral sweaters, stripes only flattering
on grandmas and little girls. Restored
from wedding starvation, I let it slip
onto my middle finger,
a perfect fit.

Sometimes the past doesn't wreck us,
but holds a splint to our halved selves,
builds the shell to protect
or for Venus to ride.

I put it back.
The loss would be too great if it fell down the drain,
or was left on the sink at work,
clattered to the bottom
of a gym locker.
It trumpets protection at home, hidden,
ensconced in the everyday safe nude briefs
its power shielded from healing everyone else, too—
I save its cerulean aegis for myself.

One and a Half Sashiko Quilts

Outside of Bethlehem PA, 2018

my mother order quarters of indigo cotton from the west coast
        sashiko means "little stabs" and would strengthen whatever it was
        woven into
    even housecoats, even armor, to hold in heat, to hold snuffing water
        some needles deposit licks of ink subcutaneous, we get matching
        hearts
the gold outlines turned bronze, then brown, somewhere leaving glitter
        rubbed onto a cheekbone, diluted with lavender laundry, mixed
        into socks
cranes, lotus, money purse, a knot for unity
        the unfinished wedding quilt was blue and white, the backing
        jacquard pearl
i disassemble thread by thread
the whole one covered every bed i've had ever since
        i lie on the office carpet, shrouded and rolled up too close to the
        electric fireplace
        or post summer shower before i start to sweat again
i lie on it like kangaroo care at the NICU
    some assembled squares sit in opaque tupperware under the
    basement ping pong table
        it will sit there until i clean out their house
now i self-swaddle, we all soften over time
        as each hole in cotton, and everything else,
        continues to widen

Haibun for Running Into Your Ex
San Francisco, 1977

"After the war, your Granny and I took care of the estate of Mr. Martin." Mrs. Martin's oil painting of her poodle still hangs across from Auntie's spot at the dining table. A bite-size Matisse wannabe, with putrid ochre and violent yellow behind tufts of thick white curled fur, the frame is gold and wide. The dog was a terror. "Mr. Martin was kind to me," who confessed to pretending to be stupid so she could be mean. Made the Japanese-demon-face behind his back. Cut her nails onto his bedsheets. Left an errant hair under his napkin, as a curse. "Granny was happy to have work." Smallness and otherness as aegis. "But when she would see her abandoned husband in the Mission District,

He would cross the street,"
look down at the sidewalk cracks.
Ghosts never have teeth.

Practical Magic

Tule Lake Relocation Center, 1945

We pass the golden eagle
statue back and forth, then hold
it between us. I am thirteen,
which must be lucky, since every-
thing they tell us is a lie. My mother
takes the cooking pot, drops
in one grain for every month
we've been here. Forty-one. With-
out rinsing, the water clouds
as starch and asbestos swirl.
We shred one page from
the dropped library book. No blood
from the student who was shot.
On each slip or square, we write
a name or place. Like twenty
questions: animal (bear), vegetable
(strawberry), mineral (iron
barbed wire). We boil it to paste,
then paint the bottom jambs
with sticky translucence. It shines
pearlescent. "During every war,
they bring food to the onibaba
on the outskirts." Even the rude
children. Even the dogs. Even
all of the women (left behind).

A Good Mix
Suburban PA, 2001

My mother confesses, "Granny says white babies
are like kittens." I match my parents, at least, for
being so mixed. In AP Biology, the punnet squares
show I am lucky to be heterozygous for blue eyes.
I am "a good mix" that blends in enough. I can stay
out of the sun. In Rome, they ask me for directions.
The family curse lives under a wolf, there. Grand-
daughter of the oldest brother. I must be blessed
to live un-usurped except for what might have been.
At sixteen, I read *The Bluest Eye* and dream of what
I would fix first. That year, we get two kittens from
the store in the mall. I always begged for a puppy
instead. They are from the same litter, but only share
the Platonic Ideal of Cat. The orange one loves me
but the tabby pisses on my bed. It doesn't matter
who you're related to, as long as you are lovable.

Etymological Triptych
San Francisco, 2009

I. I have no Japanese name.
My cousin, Albert, gets to be
Ishiro, beloved firstborn. We joke,
"The Prince." He isn't even
related by blood, hasn't earned
this attention and affection
through the same suffering. His mother
married into our line, knowing
the curse: the younger brother always
usurps the older. Jack will be
displaced, die loveless—except for his
white, pining overseas mistress.

II. Birthright
The women do not die alone. I forsake misfortune
        for my sex, assigned at birth. (They will never
see me as nonbinary.) Progeny of a mixed,
        self-proclaimed bastard, I am half of half
and wholly burdened with Shizuko's cheek bones,
        blanched almond skin (too dark to be
the desired cherry blossom). A descendent of the rising sun
        isn't special. After all, it's just another star.

III. Autogenous
Even when sensei refuses to work with girls, I practice at home. I rename
myself post-divorce back to my father, back to the first of my name. I
am the unacknowledged half of a Passover, an Internment, a doctor's
note away from the work camps, I am a miracle, lucky baby, California
terroir, East Coast terror. "First of their name" resonates, a chorus of
genes. I name myself in the umbilical cleft. I left it last year, so if you ask,
"What are you?" you should really ask "Who?" I will say I have names no
one can pronounce, but can you scream? You can settle for what my
mother gifted me and I reclaimed. "Stephanie." "Ishiro" will also do.

white like sun / dark like marrow
Suburban New Jersey, 2022

1. chiaro(scuro)

The white sides have scrubbed this history out of us like mud
and pollen on Mr. Martin's floors. A bone china dinner plate

becomes a mirror. I am thirteen when I first see myself
in San Francisco. My first California roll at ten. My mother says

she has a hole in her heart. Every mochi unsharpens its sides—
roasted rice tea washes this wound. The only way to connect

is through what becomes part of the body. The good rice
with a cartoon rosebud on glossy woven plastic. We split

the twenty-five pound bag. I add white miso to chicken soup.
It must be cellular magic, how the stomach links to the heart.

2. (chiaro)scuro

We don't know how to build an ancestral Shinto altar. Instead, the
mantel of white firebricks only holds birthday cards and
Bonnema's silver candlesticks.

We add Jack's black bear statue, a sign she forgives Oji. All these
too must hold ancestral magic from both sides, enough to break
the family curse. The sun

bleaches everything else but me. I turn from anemic cherry blossom
to bronze, something closer to steel, determined to stay just as soft
as gold.

Heavenly / Harbor
1960 / 2019

                        At
Tahoe Heavenly Valley Lodge   the Newport Harbor
Marriott
              I go in first, wiggle
    in tweed pencil skirt   in cutoff denim
        past nub-carpet, the brass bell,
        the flanking luggage racks—
        I'm eyed with gentle interest or even better:
        indifference. Outside,
Jack   my girlfriend
        waits while I get one room key. I pass back
        through the lobby to collect my
[Jap]   [dyke]
        partner. We return through to get to
        our room. This time, a gauntlet. When
        your presentation is safer as a
        potted philodendron. What beautiful
[yellow peril]   [rainbow blues]
        peace lilies flank the stairs. They are
        all fake. A part, but apart. Imposter.
Fedoras in sandstone palettes   Popped-collar pastel polos
              with hard
arms hooked around translucent necks.   Bellies like halved plastic eggs.
      What threat is here? all of us wonder
            each in our own
            clandestine ways.

Sonnet for when they ask "What are you?" at a party
Off-Campus, State University, 2004

Self-named rice cracker, off-white alien:
The Garden State deadens, renders soporific
rejected eastern roots, an unspecific
mix: make them guess the numinous origin,
question cellular levels. Bacchanalian
games measures melanin—no scientific
reason, curiosity turns the Pacific
red: I am othered, diasporic Californian.

In dreams: return to golden saccharine,
to Oakland, dry Atlantic humidity,
baptize Bay. No party games. Byzantine
here, mix is typical: "They look like me,"
in every variant, glitter amniotic. I owe
nothing, and now respond: "Fuck exotic."

~~Recipe for [Surviving] Disaster~~ Rice for Quapas

Ingredients:
1 c. Kokuho Rose Rice
16 oz. frozen, riced cauliflower
Water to rinse, filtered water to cook (about 1 ¼ c)
1 t garlic powder
1 t kosher salt
1 t herbs of choice
2 T butter

Rice cooker

Method:
1. Set your mise en place. ~~Do not think about the person who taught you this.~~
2. Rinse the rice. *Save the water to wash your hair. Add a tablespoon to the elderly dog's otherwise dry kibble.* ~~*You are a mutt.*~~ *Pour half a cup over the orchid pressed against the kitchen window—just the roots.* ~~Do not think about the family tree and the poisoned rice in the camps. Do not think about asbestos or talcum powder or stomach cancer.~~
3. Fill with enough filtered water to the right indentation. *Accept that you do not have the intuition of your mother. Guilt, however, is inheritable.*
4. Add the packet of frozen, riced cauliflower. *Like this, you are always trying to be something that you are not.*
5. Add salt, garlic powder, and herb of your choice. *There is always something French-reminiscent and fragrant growing on the deck. The grocery store jars might as well be full of pencil shavings. You were not raised like this.*
6. Top with butter. Cover. Press the button to "cook." ~~Do not scrutinize your eyes nose chin cheekbones in the lid's reflection. Do not admire them either.~~ *Hold your face eight inches above the steam. Everything either makes you prettier or older. It's your choix.*
7. Once finished, mix thoroughly and deposit in the serving vessel of your choice. *There is always something breakable. All of the heirlooms are eggshells.*
8. ~~Do not think about the soft, white hands of your Bonnema fluffing the rice for her tanned family.~~
9. *Figure out what is missing and learn to live without it.*

Grand Slam
Tacoma WA, 1939

Jack takes a baseball bat
to the river. August spawning season.
      The dry rock tops steam
like the belly of a monster cut open.
      Unlaces right boot, then
left, pulls them off without sitting and sets
      each woolen sock safely
inside. There is no one out sunning today.

Salmon bounce and skip
upstream, suddenly buoyant and silver.
      Across the frothing surface,
Jack wades in halfway amidst the frenzy.
      He winds up, tight as a fist,
smacks one out of midair toward the bank—
      it lands next to his shoes.
Not all hits are lucky. Not everyone is lucky.

Jack knows he's firstborn—
blessed. Extra pressure to provide as the sole
      sober near-adult. A quarry
of four; he will share with his sister. He escapes
      hunger and a beating
that night. No one is ever full. When he's bunted
      across the room, it's so
his little brother isn't. We can only break the cycles
      we know we're a part of.

He feels nothing for the fish struck out of the air
      like a perfect pitch. Stoic hit.
They never see it coming.

For the No-Nos
Tule Lake Relocation Center, 1943

To the tar-paper shacks, no
one could live there. Did they know
this was prison? Crickets begin a soprano
chorus, each sotto voce *pian piano.*
Each note as pentatonic domino
cascades over the Monte Casino
growing along the fence. Sterno
distributed monthly, each inferno
rekindles what's lost: grannie's kimono,
the house, a hundred pounds. Cyano
sky. Peace always before the volcano.
Every body is a composite of amino
acids, chemicals. Atomic eternity. No-
thing else persists. No-
minal freedom. No
destiny manifest. No-
where. Hydrogen. No
body. Bomb. No
more.

The War, 202X
after Ilya Kaminsky

Still (surgical) masked at Whole Foods.

Still in four brick walls and three bed-

rooms and one-and-a-half baths. We lived

(happily) because my grandparents did

not. Reparations are (checks) written

in red. This nest egg, generational wealth.

Their rice, laced with asbestos (for freshness).

They were all executed over time:

slow poison eats holes in the stomach.

The body consumes itself in war. In love,

I rinse the rice with filtered water, though

the (fluoride-supplemented) tap is

probably good enough. You can never be

too careful.

To sleep, perchance
Oakland CA, 2019

Auntie and Pepper snore baritone
on the faded loveseat, faces slack,

mouths open, each a rotated question-
mark, curled around a tasseled pillow

or Sudoku volume. Jet lag wants to
lull me supine, and I promise to fight

until at least nine. At least until
the sun goes down. The after-dinner

nature documentary flashes sepia
and grey; pachyderm thunder

would rumble the coffee table
if the volume wasn't down so low.

Yellow subtitles broadcast: "The story
of elephants shouldn't be about ivory.

It should be about their teeth." Is all life
measured by death? How many heart-

beats I have left, or who here is
the closest to unbeing? The titans

stroll past a line of skulls, touch
a tender trunk to each one. I surrender

to my own temporary slumber, and on the way
to the guest bed, cover Auntie with the lap quilt

from my mother. Pepper gets a nose pat. I wonder
what dreams may come.

They Won't Come Out
Oakland CA, 2013

Auntie circumvents direct
questions. She turns the camps

into the mild weather today, or
a sale at the fabric shop. But

when we get an Irish coffee
or share a wine tasting, she'll let the crack of light

under the doorway of memory show four students
running from the library dropping as each passes

the guard tower. Remembers the twitches and pages
flutter away, up and over the barbed wire. Or school
named by number. Or the time a neighbor accused
her of stealing a golden eagle statuette. Or beating

the bully with an umbrella for the first time to prevent
a second. Or Jack, "who suffered the most" under
his father, as the oldest, emasculated, imprisoned. We sip
something fruity from Sonoma until the last dregs

dribble onto the woven cotton placemats. The next day
these dark red spots remain; they won't come out. She didn't escape

unscathed. Jack turned into a bear with blunted horse teeth. She, into
a totem of birds, or a dragonfly mantle hovering above the lemon tree.

To sprout a lemon seed,
New Jersey, 2013

you have to free it
of its fruit. Rinsing
in a loveless sieve
will do,
                              but the best
way is to keep
            it in your mouth
for a full   three minutes,

            until each sour molecule
dissolves.   Remember

            not to swallow. Safe-
guard this   nascent

            promise. Keep turning
against your teeth, tongue-

            probe every divot until you're left
with the bitter wrinkled pit, until

this acrid hope knows its first taste
            of rain   was from you.

The Other Tree
Oakland CA, 2019

Under this ancestral sanctuary of uncollected leaves & flirting
birds, Chopin wafting from an open window—part of me is always

home here. Beneath these swollen suns, Auntie's backyard plastic-
woven chair faded to seafoam—even when it becomes bleached

in another fifty years, when who knows who of us will still be here,
the green remains. How many seeds have nestled in decomposing fruit?

Sprouted at the trunk like little weeds. Auntie sends a box every
Christmas, with Meyer lemons and rosemary from the front yard.

I'm sure the neighborhood dogs mark it as their own. We make
sure to wash it all well—their own tiny baptism. Nestled between

the softening fruits and stiff branches: five and dime trinkets, dollar store
figurines, tiny packages taped with shimmering fish stickers.

Beneath this other family tree, I re-enter the narrative. Entwine these
words like nascent roots, thread through backyard dirt and last year's

leaves. Even if she sells this house to a predatory tenant, even if this
is the last time I share the air with her and this, I will always trace my-
self back here.

Acknowledgements

"To another girl, called 'other'" was first published by *antonym lit* in 2021.

"(Re)Generation Triptych (1940-2019)" was first published in *Odes to Our Undoing*, an anthology published by St. Mary's College of California, 2022. The final section, "III. It Will Be a Garden Again (2019)" was first published separately, in Maryland Institute College of Art's journal, *FULL BLEED*, Issue 5, 2021.

"Pancakes with Ojisan" was first published in *Arriving at a Shoreline* with great weather for MEDIA, August 2022.

"'You can't say 'Oriental'" was a runner-up for the Sandy Crimmins Prize in Poetry, and appeared in *Philadelphia Stories'* Spring 2022 Issue.

"To sprout a lemon seed, (2013)" was first published in Randolph College's MFA Lit Mag, *Revolute* .003, 2022. Named a finalist for *Best of the Net* 2022.

"Something (Hidden and) Blue (Abides)" was first published by Lady Blue Literary Arts Journal, Issue 5, 2018.

"Art Imitates Life" and "Superior(ity) Complex(ion)" was first published by *Middleground Magazine*, Issue 6, 2022.

"My mother is sad today so," was first published in *West Trestle*, July 2022. "They Won't Come Out," "Only Bonnema," and "MoonShine" were first published in *White Wall Review*, 2022.

"Solidarity" was published by *Five South* in *The Weekly*, 2022.

"Auntie, Refusing Baptism," "Auntie E, Cross-Country," "Just Desserts," "One More and You're Out," "Generational Demons as Indigestion," "Haibun for Running Into Your Ex," "Après-Camp, or, Retail Therapy," "Very cruel race.," "To sleep, perchance," and "An Ode on the E" appear in *sweet euphemism*, chapbook with CLASH!, 2023.

"Inedible" was first published in *Kissing Dynamite*, Issue 47, 2022. "A Good Mix" and "[Quapa] Imposter Syndrome" were first published by *One Art*, 2023.

"Grand Slam" was first published in *Cleaver*, Issue 39, 2022.

"For the No-Nos" was first published by Moonstone Arts, and later appeared in *The Gate Memory*, Haymarket Press, 2025.

"Practical Magic" was first published in *Foglifter*, 8.1, 2023.

"Self Portrait in a Type of Mirror" was first published in *The Chestnut Review*, 4.3, 2023.

"Imposter Syndrome" and "A Good Mix" first appeared with *One Art*, 2022.

"They called my mother" and "Sonnet for when they ask, "What are you?" at a party" were first published by Quarter Press in *The Quarter(ly)* Vol. 5, 2023.

"Trompe L'oeil, le Cœur" and "The King of Horses" first appeared in *COUPLET*, 2023.

"white like sun / dark like marrow" first appeared with *Sand Hills Literary Magazine*, 2023.

"Derivative Curriculum," "Jack as Botanical Triptych," "Writing the Wrongs," "Before Any Binary," "The Real Prize Is to Know," "Before I know better," "Nothing Skips a Generation," "Parable of the Tiger," "Heavenly / Harbor," and "Love can look like" were first published in *It Skips a Generation*, chapbook with Stanchion, 2023.

"YellowThroat" won an Editor's Prize for *Philadelphia Stories'* National Poetry Contest and was published online, 2024.

"Rice for Quapas" first appeared in in *Honey Literary* #7, 2024.

Alison Lubar teaches high school English by day and yoga by night. They are a queer, nonbinary, biracial Nikkei femme whose life work has evolved into bringing mindfulness practices to young people. They're the author of two full-length poetry books, *The Other Tree*, winner of Harbor Editions' Laureate Prize (2025), and *METAMOURPHOSIS* (fifth wheel press, 2024), as well as four chapbooks: *Philosophers Know Nothing About Love* (Thirty West, 2022), *queer feast* (Bottlecap Press, 2022), *sweet euphemism* (Mouthfeel Press, 2023), and *It Skips a Generation* (Stanchion, 2023). Find out more at alisonlubar.com or on Twitter @theoriginalison.

About Small Harbor Publishing

The Other Tree is the winner of the 2023 Laureate Prize. Each year, the prize is judged by a rotating poet Laureate. The 2023 judge was Maya Williams. Previous winner of the Laureate Prize: M.T. Vallarta (2021).

Small Harbor Publishing is a 501c3 nonprofit organization. Our goal is to publish unique and diverse voices. We are a feminist press, and we are committed to diversity and inclusion. We strive to bring new voices to a devoted and expanding readership.

Small Harbor Publishing began in 2018 with the first issue of *Harbor Review*. The magazine is an online space where poetry and art converse. *Harbor Review* quickly grew and now publishes reviews and runs multiple micro chapbook competitions, including the Washburn Prize and the Editor's Prize.

In July 2020, Small Harbor Publishing was officially incorporated and began Harbor Editions. Harbor Editions accepts submissions through a chapbook open reading period, a hybrid chapbook open reading period, the Marginalia Series, and the Laureate Prize.

In 2023, Harbor Anthologies began with a mission to promote texts that explore social justice issues and highlight marginalized writers.

If you would like to support Small Harbor Publishing, visit our "About" page at: smallharborpublishing.com/about.

Alison with Mom & Auntie - Oakland, CA 2019

www.ingramcontent.com/pod-product-compliance
Lightning Source LLC
Chambersburg PA
CBHW020800130626
46554CB00006B/2278